Auditing

Workbook

John Taylor

Published by Osborne Books Limited
Unit 1B Everoak Estate
Bromyard Road, Worcester WR2 5HP
Tel 01905 748071
Email books@osbornebooks.co.uk
Website www.osbornebooks.co.uk

Design by Laura Ingham

Printed by CPI Group (UK) Limited, Croydon, CR0 4YY, on environmentally friendly, acid-free paper from managed forests.

British Library Cataloguing in Publication Data
A catalogue record for this book is available from the British Library

ISBN 978 1909173 378

Contents

Acknowledgements

The publisher wishes to thank the following for their help with the reading and production of the book: Jon Moore, Bee Pugh and Cathy Turner. Thanks are also due to Jo Osborne for her technical reading and Laura Ingham for her designs for this series.

The publisher is indebted to the Association of Accounting Technicians for its help and advice to our author and editor during the preparation of this text.

Author and Technical Editor

John Taylor is a Chartered Accountant who spent many years in professional practice, advising small and medium-sized businesses before becoming the Financial Director of a Leeds based public limited company. In 2004 John joined the staff of Leeds Metropolitan University, where he specialises in teaching management accounting and auditing on a range of professional courses.

Jo Osborne is a Chartered Accountant who trained with Ernst & Young in their London office. She then moved to Cable & Wireless where she spent two years in their internal audit department before moving into an investment appraisal role. Jo has taught AAT at Hillingdon College and until recently at Worcester College of Technology where she took on the role of AAT Coordinator.

Introduction

what this book covers

This book has been written to cover the 'External auditing' Unit which is an optional Unit for the revised (2013) AAT Level 4 Diploma in Accounting.

what this book contains

This book is set out in two sections:

- **Chapter Activities** which provide extra practice material in addition to the activities included in the Osborne Books Tutorial text. Answers to the Chapter activities are included in this book.

- **Practice Assessments** are provided to prepare the student for the Computer Based Assessments. They are based directly on the structure, style and content of the sample assessment material provided by the AAT at www.aat.org.uk. Suggested answers to the Practice Assessments are set out in this book.

further information

If you want to know more about our products and resources, please visit www.osbornebooks.co.uk for further details and access to our online shop.

Chapter activities

1   Introduction to auditing

1.1   From the list below select which of these statements best describes the reason why auditors should be independent of their clients.

		✔
(a)	They can charge larger fees as independent consultants	
(b)	The government insists auditors must be independent	
(c)	It enables them to carry out their audit without being influenced by their client	
(d)	Auditors are required to contribute to control procedures designed to detect fraud	

1.2   Decide whether each of the following statements about the role of the auditor is true or false.

		True	False
(a)	The role of the auditor is to prepare and express an opinion on the truth and fairness of a client's financial statements		
(b)	The role of the auditor is to express an opinion to the shareholders on the truth and fairness of a set of financial statements		
(c)	Auditors are responsible for detecting fraud in a set of financial statements		
(d)	The role of the auditor is to express an opinion to the directors on the truth and fairness of a set of financial statements		

1.3   State whether the following statements are true or false.

✔

		True	False
(a)	The auditor has to obtain reasonable assurance that the financial statements are true and fair		
(b)	Directors are responsible for the organisation's system of internal control which should be capable of detecting significant fraud or error		
(c)	The auditors are appointed until the end of the Annual General Meeting when they can be reappointed by the directors		
(d)	Any qualified accountant can apply to be registered as an auditor		

1.4   Who appoints the auditors?

✔

(a)	The Registrar of Companies	
(b)	An Audit Committee of non-executive directors	
(c)	The Board of Directors	
(d)	The members of the company	

2 Auditing – the legal framework

2.1 State whether the following statements are true or false in respect of the liability of auditors.

		True	False
(a)	Auditors are only responsible to shareholders		
(b)	Auditors have a duty of care towards investors or potential investors they are aware of before they sign the auditor's report		
(c)	Auditors owe a duty of care to each individual investor they are aware of before they sign the auditor's report		

2.2 Complete the following description of quality control procedures by filling in the gaps with terms from the list below:

- Regular
- Hot
- Cold
- Quality
- Ethical
- Independence
- Audit
- Reviewed
- Simple
- Complex

All audit firms must have a system of . . . . control. This should include confirmation

that . . . . standards have been maintained, that the firm's . . . . from

the client has not been compromised, that all audit work carried out has been reviewed and that the

client continues to be acceptable. A . . . . review should take place where the audit

is large or. . . . . and a system of . . . . reviews implemented to ensure

the firm's audit procedures have been adhered to.

2.3 State whether the following statements are true or false in respect of the rights of auditors.

✔

		True	False
(a)	Auditors have the right to be present at the Annual General Meeting		
(b)	Auditors have the right to have all reasonable inquiries answered		
(c)	Auditors have the right to attend all meetings of the company		
(d)	Auditors have the right to inspect any information including information not related to the financial records, for example, personnel files		
(e)	Auditors have the right to call an Annual General Meeting		

2.4 Auditors can minimise their liability to third parties in several ways.

State whether the following ways for auditors to minimise their liability is allowed or not allowed under the ethical guidelines.

✔

		Allowed	Not allowed
(a)	Auditors can include a disclaimer in their report to disclaim all liability for loss as the directors are responsible for the content		
(b)	Audit firms can operate as companies with limited liability		
(c)	Audit firms can make agreements with individual shareholders and repay any losses they have incurred in the hope that not all shareholders will claim		
(d)	Auditors can include a disclaimer in their report to disclaim all liability for loss in respect of any third party apart from the shareholders		
(e)	Audit firms can agree a maximum amount of liability with the directors and shareholders of a client		

3 Planning the audit assignment

3.1   Match each of the control activities/procedures listed below with the appropriate type of internal control shown in the table.

Control activity/procedure:

- Staff responsible for recording cash received are not responsible for processing sales invoices
- Supervisory responsibilities are clearly defined
- A requirement for two signatures on all company cheques
- Matching of sales invoices to delivery notes and original sales order
- Limited access and password protection to the payroll system

Internal control:	Control activity/procedure:
Segregation of duties	
Physical control	
Arithmetical and accounting checks	
Organisational controls	
Authorisation controls	

3.2 When planning an audit the auditors must consider audit risk and the probability of a material misstatement or error not being detected by the client's internal procedures.

Select whether the following factors are likely to increase/reduce or have no effect on audit risk.

✔

		Increase	Reduce	No effect
(a)	The company exceeds its overdraft limit every month			
(b)	The company has introduced a bonus scheme for directors based on achieving revenue and profit targets			
(c)	The company has upgraded its payroll software			
(d)	Another firm of accountants has been approached to carry out internal audit reviews			
(e)	The Audit Manager has joined the company as Financial Director			

3.3 Accounting systems should be designed with both control objectives and control procedures. Control procedures are designed to reduce the risk that control objectives are not met.

For each of the items below identify whether it is a control objective, a risk, or a control procedure.

		Control objective	Risk	Control procedure
(a)	An aged receivables analysis is prepared monthly			
(b)	Invoices can be paid before goods are delivered			
(c)	Goods are only purchased from approved suppliers			
(d)	The payroll department is notified of starters and leavers by the personnel office			
(e)	The person responsible for collecting cash from vending machines pays the cash into the bank and notifies the cashiers department of the amount collected			

3.4 When documenting a client's systems the auditors are concerned with identifying which accounting systems will be subject to audit procedures.

Glitterball Ltd manufactures jewellery for the fashion accessories market. It uses designs from independent designers and produces items in bulk for the cheaper jewellery high street retailers and accessory shops. It does not sell to the public.

Which of Glitterball's systems will not be subject to detailed audit procedures?

		✔
(a)	Purchases and supplier payments	
(b)	Inventory despatch and invoicing	
(c)	Payroll standard cost analysis	
(d)	Receivables and cash recording	

4 Audit testing

4.1 Auditors use a mixture of tests of control and substantive procedures when gathering audit evidence.

For each of the procedures below indicate whether it is a test of control, or a substantive procedure.

		Test of control	Substantive procedure
(a)	Carry out analytical review of trade payables ledger balances		
(b)	Test a sample of purchase orders for authorisation		
(c)	Reperform the bank reconciliation at year end		
(d)	Look for evidence that goods are despatched only to credit-worthy customers		
(e)	Check authorisation of new employees details added to payroll		

4.2 Auditors use sampling as part of their auditing procedures.

You are reviewing the audit programme for the audit of Bolington Ltd. The audit programme sets out the following audit tests:

From the information given decide if the test is valid or not valid.

		Valid	Not valid
(a)	Select a sample of sales invoices and credit notes and vouch with goods outwards documents		
(b)	At the inventory count identify a selection of items to be counted independently by the audit team		
(c)	To test payroll transactions check all entries in week 23		
(d)	Using random number tables select a sample of goods received notes and check to purchase invoices		

4.3   Auditors must document their procedures and have evidence that they have planned their audit and carried out sufficient testing to support their audit opinion. All their work must be documented.

From the information below decide if the documentation should be retained on the Permanent Audit file or Current Audit file.

✔

		Current file	Permanent file
(a)	Audit points forward from prior years		
(b)	Schedule of additions to non-current assets		
(c)	Copy of the client's customer list		
(d)	Analytical comparison of the client's results for previous five accounting periods		
(e)	List of client employees authorised to sign purchase orders and their authorisation limits		

4.4   An external auditor is required to carry out audit testing to gather evidence to support their conclusions.

Select whether each of the statements below is true or false.

✔

		True	False
(a)	The principle of substance over form means that auditors will examine what a transaction really is, not what it appears to be		
(b)	Auditors must use sampling techniques to test every aspect of the financial statements when auditing a large company		
(c)	Auditors should not attempt to develop a working relationship with client staff as this might compromise their independence		
(d)	Tolerable misstatement is the level of error the auditors will accept in a sample and is set lower than performance materiality		

5 Auditing accounting systems

5.1 As part of their audit work auditors will seek to verify the assertions relevant to the transactions being audited.

You are carrying out the audit of a client's payroll system. For each of the audit procedures set out below select the assertion for which the test will provide assurance.

Test	Assertion
Check a sample of new employees' details with personnel records	Existence/Classification/Accuracy/Occurrence
Check the calculations of a sample of gross pay for hourly paid employees	Occurrence/Valuation/Classification/Accuracy
Reconcile the wages control account	Cut off/Valuation/Classification/ Occurrence

5.2 Two types of computer-assisted audit techniques (CAAT) used by auditors are test data and audit interrogation software.

For each of the audit procedures listed below, select the type of CAAT which would be used to perform that procedure.

		Test data	Audit interrogation software
(a)	Stratification of ledger balances to provide data for sampling tests		
(b)	Input employee salary data to generate predicted payroll figures		
(c)	Identify any gaps in the sequence of sales invoice numbers		

5.3 The following is a description of a payroll system within Skye Ltd.

For each part of the system identify whether the procedure is a strength or a weakness or is neither a strength nor a weakness.

✔

	Strength	Neither	Weakness
(a) Each hourly paid employee is required to swipe an electronic card which records the time they enter and leave the premises. There is no supervision of this procedure.			
(b) Each departmental manager receives a printout of their employees recorded hours on the last day of the pay period and is required to initial to approve payment of those hours.			
(c) Information from the swipe card machine is downloaded automatically into the payroll programme. The Payroll Clerk can amend this manually if a manager has refused to authorise hours worked.			
(d) The Payroll Clerk can amend monthly paid employee's pay details and also all employee's deductions maintained in the payroll master file.			
(e) The Human Resources department sends an email detailing new starters and employees leaving to the Payroll Supervisor. He is responsible for ensuring that all new employees' details are input into the master file and all leavers are removed from the payroll after their final salary payment.			
(f) A BACS payment list is prepared from the payroll details and sent to the Finance Director for approval. She signs it and it is then countersigned by the Financial Controller.			
(g) All employees are paid by electronic transfer directly into their bank account.			
(h) The payroll department sends a monthly email to the accounts department showing the amounts of PAYE and NI to be paid to HM Revenue & Customs.			

5.4   Auditors use both substantive and compliance testing as part of their audit procedures.

For each of the tests described below decide whether it is a test of control or a substantive test.

	Test of control	Substantive procedure
(a) Check for evidence that supplier's accounts in the Trade Payables Ledger are reconciled monthly to the statements from the supplier		
(b) Check for evidence that purchase invoices are batched before being input into the financial records and that batch details are recorded		
(c) Check that there are no gaps in the numerical sequence of Goods Returned Notes		
(d) Check that staff leaving the client's employment are removed from the payroll promptly		
(e) Physically inspect a sample of motor vehicles and record all relevant details		

6 **Verification of assets and liabilities**

6.1   An external auditor is required to carry out audit testing to gather evidence to support their conclusions.

Select whether each of the statements below is true or false.

		True	False
(a)	If the bank reconciliation is correct there is no need for a separate confirmation letter from the bank		
(b)	Inspecting non-current assets is a valid test for existence and ownership		
(c)	Research expenditure can be capitalised as a tangible non-current asset but must be written off within five years		
(d)	Carrying out a trade receivables circularisation will provide some good evidence of existence and valuation of trade receivables balances		

6.2 The following is a description of an inventory count within Whisper Ltd.

For each part of the system identify whether the procedure is a strength or a weakness.

✔

	Strength	Weakness
(a) The count is to be carried out by Whisper staff in teams of two		
(b) One person will count the inventory and the other will record the count on a pad. Counters should bring a pad and pens for this purpose		
(c) Once counted each item should be marked with a red sticker. If teams run out of red stickers they are able to use the green ones also		
(d) The stores area has been organised into sections and each team will be allocated to a section to count		
(e) The stores staff will oversee the count and allocate teams to each area		
(f) Teams should inspect each inventory item for evidence of damage. Damaged inventory should be noted separately by each team		
(g) Where inventory is boxed staff carrying out the count are empowered to require stores staff to open a sample of the boxes to confirm the contents		
(h) Members of the audit team will observe the inventory count. They will perform their own count of a sample of items and will record them separately. Count teams must not use the auditors as additional counters		
(i) Once the inventory count is complete the count sheets should be left with Mr Brown the Stores Manager who will forward them to the finance department		

6.3   All audit working papers must be reviewed during the course of the audit.

You are the audit manager of Tickett & Wrunne and you are reviewing the audit working papers on the current audit of Snodgrass Ltd. The audit team has created a list of queries on which they would like a decision from you.

- Profit from operations is £2.4m and the auditors have set a level of performance materiality at 5% of profit from operations.

- A provision for a loss on a long-term contract has been omitted amounting to £50,000. The total value of inventory is £5m.

- The company has failed to make a provision against a trade receivables balance which may not be recoverable. The auditors calculate that it should be £25,000. The total value of trade receivables is £695,000.

- The company has classified £2.5m of leased property as freehold property.

- Expenditure on research should be written off in the year. Instead the company has treated research expenditure amounting to £15,000 as an intangible non-current asset, claiming it relates to a potential future product.

You are asked to consider which of the following is the right course of action to take when discussing these points with the client:

		✔
(a)	All the adjustments are material so all should be adjusted	
(b)	None of the adjustments are material so none need to be adjusted	
(c)	The provision against the contract in progress must be made and the property must be reclassified but no other adjustment needs to be made	
(d)	Only the provision against the work-in-progress needs to be amended	
(e)	The total of the errors exceeds the performance materiality and so all errors must be adjusted	

6.4   The external auditor should undertake analytical procedures as part of the planning process in order to identify the risk of misstatement of figures in the financial statements. The results of the analytical procedures conducted on trade receivables and trade payables in the financial statements of an audit client are listed below.

Select whether the results of these analytical procedures indicate that trade receivables and trade payables for the current year may have been under or overstated.

The results show that, compared to the previous year:

- Trade receivables have increased by 5% and revenue has increased by 15%

Understated / Overstated

- Trade payables have increased by 9% and purchases have decreased by 12%

Understated / Overstated

7   Audit completion and audit reporting

7.1   You are reviewing the audit files of Monty Ltd with a view to finalising the audit. From your review you identify the following factors. For each point decide whether or not they:

- can be ignored
- require the financial statements to be amended
- require a note in the financial statements, without any adjustment to the figures

In the table below tick the response you feel is the most appropriate.

	Ignore	Amend financial statements	Include in a note
(a) A customer owing £130,000 has gone into liquidation after the year-end and no amounts will be recovered. Total receivables amount to £1.8m and the profit from operations for the year is £750,000			
(b) Since the year end the company has issued shares to the value of £1m			
(c) Audit investigations have indicated that the latest position on one of its long-term contracts in progress shows that it is likely to make a profit of £200,000. The contract is approximately 70% completed. The value of long-term work in progress is £5m and the profit from operations for the year is £750,000			
(d) The bank financing arrangements were revised and renewed shortly after the year-end. There were no changes to previous arrangements except an increase in the client's overdraft limit of £500,000			
(e) The company had revalued its freehold properties in line with general increases in market prices but during the year the value of commercial properties fell. The auditors estimate that these properties are overvalued by approximately £300,000			
(f) After the year-end the main factory burned down causing production to stop completely. The company arranged for production to be carried out by sub-contractors whilst the factory was being rebuilt and submitted an insurance claim for its losses			

7.2 All audit working papers must be reviewed by a more senior member of the audit team during the course of an audit.

The Audit Manager is reviewing the audit working papers during the current audit of Snodgrass Ltd. The audit is for the year ended 31 March 201X. She has identified a list of points raised by audit staff and now has to decide whether or not to investigate them further.

For each of the points listed below decide whether it should be investigated further.

✔

		Investigate	Do not investigate
(a)	The company has decided to close its factory in South Wales after the year-end with the loss of 120 jobs		
(b)	On 1 March 201X the company sold all its buildings to Megabank plc, a finance company, and leased them back on a fifty year lease		
(c)	The development project number 20R4 on which the company has already spent £258,000 has been abandoned as unworkable as the proposed product could not be manufactured economically		
(d)	The audit senior had queried whether it was correct that the sums receivable under a five year contract for the supply of component parts to a major customer has been included in revenues all in one year		
(e)	The company issued new shares on 2 April 201X		

7.3   You are reviewing the audit files following completion of the audit for three clients and find that the audit files contain the points below.

For each client indicate whether or not you would recommend a modified audit report and, if so, on what basis.

Whoo Ltd

The auditors were appointed after the end of the financial year and discovered that the client had also changed banks shortly after the year-end. The directors of Whoo Ltd refused permission for the auditors to contact their previous bankers for confirmation of the year-end bank balance. They gave no reason for this refusal. The total of net current assets was £1.2m including the bank balance which was £123,000 overdrawn.

		✔
(a)	Not modified	
Modified:		
(b)	'Except for' – limitation of audit scope	
(c)	'Except for' – material disagreement	
(d)	Disclaimer – pervasive limitation of audit scope	
(e)	Adverse opinion – pervasive disagreement	

Floo Ltd

The client has discovered a long-term fraud perpetrated by the Financial Director. The amount stolen was believed to be of the order of £750,000. He had been prosecuted and jailed and legal action had commenced for recovery. The company was fully insured against fraud, so will not suffer any loss. However, the directors feel that the situation should be fully disclosed to the shareholders.

		✔
(a)	Not modified	
Modified:		
(b)	'Except for' limitation of audit scope	
(c)	'Except for' material disagreement	
(d)	Disclaimer – pervasive limitation of audit scope	
(e)	Adverse opinion – pervasive disagreement	

Bloo Ltd

The auditors have discovered that the company has invoiced several of its customers in full for services which they had agreed to supply over a period of two years. The whole of these amounts, totalling approximately £800,000 had been included in revenue for the current year. In addition Bloo Ltd has failed to make provision against two trade receivables balances amounting to £250,000 in total. The auditors have also indicated that inventory has been overvalued by approximately £300,000. This is because the directors have revalued old inventory to its current cost price. The profit from operations of Bloo Ltd is currently stated as £3.1m and the net asset value at £12.5m.

The directors have made provision in the accounts for directors' bonuses totalling £1m and are refusing to amend the financial statements for any of the points raised by the auditors.

		✔
(a)	Not modified	
Modified:		
(b)	'Except for' – limitation of audit scope	
(c)	'Except for' – material disagreement	
(d)	Disclaimer – pervasive limitation of audit scope	
(e)	Adverse opinion – pervasive disagreement	

7.4 The audit team at FluffyCo Ltd, a manufacturer of toys and games, have noted several points which they have brought to the attention of you, the audit partner. These include:

- FluffyCo Ltd's product range has not changed in the last five years and newer products are appearing on the market which are in direct competition with FluffyCo Ltd's own products

- The management of FluffyCo Ltd has not replaced their head of marketing who has left the company to join a competitor

- The bank has refused to increase FluffyCo Ltd's overdraft and has turned down its application for a loan for new equipment

- Orders from two of its key customers have declined steadily over the past year and sales volumes are dropping. The directors have pointed out that revenue is the same as the previous year, however the auditors pointed out that this is due to price rises rather than the volume of sales

- The audit team reviewed the future budgets and cash flows of FluffyCo Ltd which was prepared by the directors. They concluded that, whilst some of the assumptions were optimistic the overall projections were not unreasonable

There are no other points raised during the audit that give any indication that the financial statements are incorrect. The audit process was carried out satisfactorily.

You must now decide whether any of the above issues affect the audit opinion for the year. Indicate in the table below which course of action is the most appropriate in the circumstances.

		✔
(a)	The company is likely to be in financial trouble so a modified audit report on the financial statements should be issued on the basis that it is not a going concern	
(b)	None of these points are of significance to the financial statements and it is not the responsibility of the auditors to tell the directors what to do, so no action is required	
(c)	None of these points is significant to the financial statements for the current year. However they indicate a worrying trend which should be discussed with the directors after the audit is finalised	
(d)	The audit team should go back to FluffyCo Ltd and try to gather further audit evidence that the company is not a going concern so that the audit report can be modified	

Chapter activities
answers

1 Introduction to auditing

1.1 (c) It enables them to carry out their audit without being influenced by their client

1.2 **(b)** The role of the auditor is to express an opinion to the shareholders on the truth and fairness of a client's financial statements

1.3 **(a)** True

(b) True

(c) False – auditors are reappointed by the shareholders

(d) False – only members of one of the Recognised Supervisory Bodies can carry out external audits

1.4 (d) The members of the company

2   Auditing – the legal framework

2.1 **(a)**   False – auditors also have a responsibility to potential investors they are aware of

(b)   True

(c)   False – auditors are only liable to investors collectively

2.2   All audit firms must have a system of **quality** control. This should include confirmation that **ethical** standards have been maintained, that the firm's **independence** from the client has not been compromised, that all audit work carried out has been reviewed and that the client continues to be acceptable. A **hot** review should take place where the audit is large or **complex** and a system of **cold** reviews implemented to ensure the firm's audit procedures have been adhered to.

2.3 **(a)**   True

(b)   True

(c)   False – they have a right only if the meeting relates to their appointment

(d)   True

(e)   False

2.4

		Allowed	Not allowed
(a)	Auditors can include a disclaimer in their report to disclaim all liability for loss as the directors are responsible for the content		✔
(b)	Audit firms can operate as companies with limited liability	✔	
(c)	Audit firms can make agreements with individual shareholders and repay any losses they have incurred in the hope that not all shareholders will claim		✔
(d)	Auditors can include a disclaimer in their report to disclaim all liability for loss in respect of any third party apart from the shareholders		✔
(e)	Audit firms can agree a maximum amount of liability with the directors and shareholders of a client	✔	

3 Planning the audit assignment

3.1

Internal control:	Control activity/procedure:
Segregation of duties	Staff responsible for recording cash received are not responsible for processing sales invoices
Physical control	Limited access and password protection to the payroll system
Arithmetical and accounting checks	Matching of sales invoices to delivery notes and original sales order
Organisational controls	Supervisory responsibilities are clearly defined
Authorisation controls	A requirement for two signatures on all company cheques

3.2

		Increase	Reduce	No effect
(a)	The company exceeds its overdraft limit every month	✔		
(b)	The company has introduced a bonus scheme for directors based on achieving revenue and profit targets	✔		
(c)	The company has upgraded its payroll software		✔	
(d)	Another firm of accountants has been approached to carry out internal audit reviews		✔	
(e)	The Audit Manager has joined the company as Financial Director			✔

3.3

		Control objective	Risk	Control procedure
(a)	An aged receivables analysis is prepared monthly			✔
(b)	Invoices can be paid before goods are delivered		✔	
(c)	Goods are only purchased from approved suppliers	✔		
(d)	The payroll department is notified of starters and leavers by the personnel office			✔
(e)	The person responsible for collecting cash from vending machines pays the cash into the bank and notifies the cashiers department of the amount collected		✔	

3.4   (c)   Payroll standard cost analysis

4 Audit testing

4.1

		Test of control	Substantive procedure
(a)	Carry out analytical review of trade payables ledger balances		✔
(b)	Test a sample of purchase orders for authorisation	✔	
(c)	Reperform the bank reconciliation at year-end		✔
(d)	Look for evidence that goods are despatched only to credit-worthy customers	✔	
(e)	Check authorisation of new employees' details added to payroll	✔	

4.2   (a), (b) and (d) are valid; (c) is not valid

4.3

		Current file	Permanent file
(a)	Audit points forward from prior years	✔	
(b)	Schedule of additions to non-current assets	✔	
(c)	Copy of the client's customer list		✔
(d)	Analytical comparison of the client's results for previous five accounting periods	✔	
(e)	List of client employees authorised to sign purchase orders and their authorisation limits		✔

4.4   (a) and (d) are true; (b) and (c) are false

5   Auditing accounting systems

5.1

Test	Assertion
Check a sample of new employees details with personnel records	Existence
Check the calculations of a sample of gross pay for hourly paid employees	Accuracy
Reconcile the wages control account	Classification

5.2

		Test data	Audit interrogation software
(a)	Stratification of ledger balances to provide data for sampling tests		✔
(b)	Input employee salary data to generate predicted payroll figures	✔	
(c)	Identify any gaps in the sequence of sales invoice numbers		✔

5.3   (b), (f) and (g) are strengths; (a), (d) and (e) are weaknesses; (c) and (h) are neither.

5.4

		Test of control	Substantive procedure
(a)	Check for evidence that supplier's accounts in the Trade Payables Ledger are reconciled monthly to the statement from the supplier	✔	
(b)	Check for evidence that purchase invoices are batched before being input into the financial records and that batch details are recorded	✔	
(c)	Check that there are no gaps in the numerical sequence of Goods Returned Notes	✔	
(d)	Check that staff leaving the client's employment are removed from the payroll promptly		✔
(e)	Physically inspect a sample of motor vehicles and record all relevant details		✔

6 Verification of assets and liabilities

6.1 (a), (b) and (c) are false; (d) is true.

6.2 (a), (d), (f), (g) and (h) are strengths; (b), (c), (e) and (i) are weaknesses.

6.3 (c) The provision against the contract in progress must be made and the property must be reclassified but no other adjustment needs be made.

6.4 • Trade receivables has increased by 5% and revenue has increased by 15%

Understated

• Trade payables have increased by 9% and purchases have decreased by 12%

Overstated

7 Audit completion and audit reporting

7.1   (a) and (e) – Amend financial statements; (c) and (d) – Ignore; (b) and (f) – Include in a note.

7.2   Investigate (b), (c) and (d); Do not investigate (a) and (e).

7.3   **Whoo Ltd**

(b)   'Except for' – limitation of audit scope

Floo Ltd

(a)   Not modified

Bloo Ltd

(e)   Adverse opinion – pervasive disagreement

7.4   (c)   None of these points is significant to the financial statements for the current year. However they indicate a worrying trend which should be discussed with the directors after the audit is finalised

Practice
assessment 1

Task 1

When carrying out an external audit it is very important that the auditors have a clear understanding of the internal controls within the client's accounting system. Segregation of duties is a fundamental principle of internal control in order to ensure:

✔

(a)	Employees cannot collude together to commit fraud	
(b)	No one person has complete control of any aspect of the accounting function	
(c)	No one individual can control the processing of a transaction from start to finish	
(d)	It is difficult to conceal errors or frauds	

Choose **one** option.

Task 2

The following are procedures that are carried out within the sales system of Bugle Ltd.

For each procedure, decide whether it is a strength or a weakness.

✔

		Strength	Weakness
(a)	Sales invoices are processed by James who also banks any monies received from customers		
(b)	The sales order processing department telephones customer orders through to the despatch department which then delivers the goods to customers together with a delivery note		
(c)	Customers are not sent monthly statements. James is responsible for collecting overdue debts and issuing credit notes where necessary		

Task 3

The external auditor may seek to place reliance on internal controls in order to restrict the amount of substantive testing.

In each of the following circumstances, decide whether the external auditor is likely to be able to place reliance on the internal control.

✔

		Reliance	No reliance
(a)	A client with an independent internal audit department		
(b)	A family company where the Financial Director and the Chief Executive are related		
(c)	A company where a fraud committed by the Purchasing Manager has been uncovered		

Task 4

Auditors are required to give either limited or reasonable assurance.

Decide which of these assignments would be one where reasonable assurance is required?

Select **one** option.

		✔
(a)	Assignment to review a client's cash flow forecast on behalf of a bank	
(b)	Assignment to prepare financial statements from information provided by the client	
(c)	Assignment to carry out a review of the client's internal control systems and report on behalf of the management	
(d)	None of the above	

Task 5

External auditors use a variety of methods for documenting systems of control, including flowcharts, internal control questionnaires (ICQs), and narrative notes.

You are the Audit Manager documenting a client's accounting systems. Decide which is the most appropriate way of documenting a client's accounting systems for each of the following situations.

	Flowchart	Narrative notes	ICQ
(a) Documenting the purchases system with internal controls clearly indicated			
(b) Making enquiries of client staff about the day-to-day operations			
(c) Identifying possible areas where fraud could be committed within the payroll system			

Task 6

An external auditor is required to obtain an understanding of the control environment within an audited entity.

Select whether each of the following factors contributes to a strong control environment, a weak control environment, or has no effect.

	Strong	Weak	No effect
(a) The organisation has an internal audit department that reports to the Finance Director			
(b) Management takes the view that office staff are costly so staff levels in the accounts department are kept to a minimum			
(c) The Finance Director is a qualified accountant who has been with the company for twenty years and was previously the Financial Controller			
(d) The external auditors carry out extensive substantive testing of balances in the Statement of Financial Position			

Task 7

Accounting systems have control objectives and control procedures to mitigate the risks that the control objective is not met.

For each of the following, select whether they are a control objective, risk, or control procedure.

	Control objective	Risk	Control procedure
(a) Organisations sell goods or services to customers with poor credit ratings			
(b) Goods are purchased only from approved suppliers			
(c) All purchase invoices must be matched to purchase orders and goods received notes			

Task 8

The following are descriptions of procedures within the revenue and receivables system of an audit client.

Indicate which of these procedures might be a significant weakness that should be communicated to the management of the client.

Choose all that apply.

✔

Procedure	
(a)	Customers' outstanding balances are not checked against their credit limits before new sales orders are accepted	
(b)	Goods delivered to customers are accompanied by two copies of the Delivery Note. One is signed by the customer and is retained in the Despatch Department, the other is retained by the customer	
(c)	Orders from customers can be placed by telephone or in writing. Telephone orders are recorded on an Internal Order pad and a copy is sent to the Accounts Department and the Despatch Department. The pad does not indicate who took the order and it is not signed	
(d)	An aged receivables analysis is prepared monthly and used by the Credit Control Department to chase payment of invoices where the customer has failed to comply with the credit terms	

Task 9

The figures below are a summary of an analytical review of the draft financial statements of Howdo Ltd. The review was carried out at the planning stage and the comparison was made against the original budget for the financial year.

Based on the results of this analytical review indicate whether or not you would investigate or accept the reason for any differences.

		Actual	**Budget**	**Investigate**	**Accept**
(a)	Gross profit	56%	64%		
(b)	Profit for the year margin	12%	14%		
(c)	Trade Receivables days	38 days	42 days		
(d)	Trade Payables days	36 days	49 days		
(e)	Inventory turnover	9 times	12 times		

Task 10

Auditors use samples in their audit testing. Decide in which of the following situations is the use of sampling not appropriate:

Select **one** option.

(a)	When the population is homogenous	
(b)	When all items in the population have an equal chance of being selected	
(c)	When the population is very small and all the items are material	
(d)	When the population consists of a large number of transactions	

Task 11

External auditors use analytical procedures, tests of control and tests of detail to gather audit evidence.

Identify whether each of the following procedures is an analytical procedure, a test of control or a test of detail.

Procedure	Analytical procedure	Test of control	Test of detail
(a) Check a sample of overtime payments to ensure they have been authorised			
(b) A comparison of percentage increases or decreases in distribution costs from period to period			
(c) Vouch a sample of sales orders to delivery notes			

Task 12

As part of their testing to verify revenues an auditor will inspect sales invoices. The auditor will gain assurance about different assertions depending on the information included in the invoice.

For each piece of information below, select **one** assertion for which it will provide assurance.

	Accuracy	Classification	Cut-off	Existence
(a) Date of the invoice				
(b) Description of the item sold				
(c) Monetary amount				

Task 13

Jellybean Ltd is a manufacturer of sweets and confectionery. It purchases raw materials including sugar, colouring, syrups and flavour enhancers in bulk quantities. Sweets and confectionery are sold in boxes and bags. Jellybean Ltd sells its own 'Suckitandsee' range and also makes confectionery and sweets for other retailers which are sold under their brand names.

You are to set out, in a manner suitable for inclusion in the audit plan, the audit procedures to be undertaken in order to ensure that inventory of raw material and finished goods are fairly stated in the financial statements.

Task 14

The audit work to be carried out requires the verification of cut-off procedures to ensure that all transactions are recorded in the correct accounting period.

During the year-end inventory count on 31 March 201X the audit team recorded the following transactions.

The last Goods Received Note number issued in the year was 10672.

Below is a list of invoices received around the year end. Decide which invoices should be recorded in purchases for the year.

Select **one** option from the second table below.

Invoice no. ref	Supplier	Invoice date	GRN number	Amount
95493	Big Trumpet plc	28 March	10674	£3,098.45
95494	Last Post Ltd	31 March	10671	£12,274.20
94495	Bugle Ltd	29 March	10673	£1,567.90
94496	Bangalong Ltd	30 March	10672	£12,786.42
94497	Simbol plc	1 April	10670	£456.48
94498	Twangalong Ltd	31 March	10675	£998.46

	✔
(a) All of them except 94497 as this is dated after the year-end	
(b) 95494, 94496 and 94497	
(c) 95493, 95494 and 94496	
(d) 95493, 95494, 94495 and 94496	

Task 15

Two types of computer-assisted audit techniques (CAAT) are test data and audit software.

For each of the procedures listed below, select the type of CAAT which would be used to perform that procedure.

		Test data	Audit software
(a)	Select all sales ledger accounts showing a credit balance for review		
(b)	Input of issues of inventory in excess of balance of inventory items available as shown on inventory system		
(c)	Select all accounts in the receivables (sales) ledger where the balance owed exceeds credit limit		

Task 16

The auditor's assessment of the integrity of management is a key aspect of planning an audit and assessing audit risk.

As part of the audit planning the auditor should consider whether the attitude of management is likely to increase or decrease the risk of a weak control environment.

For each of the comments made by management below indicate whether it will increase or decrease the risk.

Management comment		Increase risk	Decrease risk
(a)	'We have appointed a new head of internal audit who is a qualified accountant'		
(b)	'We have had to cut back on accounts staff due to the economic situation so they are all covering several tasks'		
(c)	'We are not bothering with a stock count this year – we will use the computer figures'		

Task 17

The objective of a substantive test will determine the population from which the sample for testing is selected.

For each of the objectives set out below, select the population from which the sample should be selected.

(a)   Obtain evidence of the existence of inventories

> **Inventory records / Inventory count**

(b)   Obtain evidence that the client only purchases the goods it needs

> **Purchase orders / Purchase invoices**

Task 18

Select whether the following statements in respect of an external auditor's working papers are true or false.

	True	False
(a) The auditors must be able to show they have gathered evidence to substantiate their audit opinion		
(b) All audit working papers should show evidence of review		
(c) The Permanent File contains the audit programme to be followed and all the background data for the client		

Task 19

The errors listed below have been identified during the audit of BiggBatt Ltd. The directors of BiggBatt Ltd refuse to make adjustments to correct the errors.

The audit firm Tickett & Wrunne set a performance materiality level of 5% of net profit for the year before tax as the yardstick to determine whether errors are material. BiggBatt Ltd's profit before tax is £250,000.

Select whether each of the following errors must be adjusted in order that Tickett & Wrunne can issue an unmodified audit opinion on the financial statements.

(**Note** – examples are individual, not cumulative)

		Requires to be adjusted	Does not require to be adjusted
(a)	An overstatement of trade receivables amounting to £7,000, and an understatement of trade payables amounting to £4,800		
(b)	Incorrect depreciation calculations resulting in it being understated by £9,000 and an overstatement of inventory amounting to £6,400		
(c)	Understatement of director's bonuses of £10,000		

Task 20

Often one of the most significant costs incurred by an organisation is its staff costs.

Some of the key internal control objectives in respect of payroll are:

- Ensure that only bona fide employees are paid
- Ensure that all master data is correct and that any amendments are properly made
- Ensure that all employees are paid the correct amounts
- Ensure that all employees are paid in the correct period
- Ensure that any deductions from payroll are properly made
- Ensure that amounts due to outside organisations (HMRC, pension funds etc) are paid at the correct time

Set out in a manner suitable for inclusion in an audit programme the procedures to be followed when auditing a client's payroll system.

Task 21

Which **two** of these purchase invoices should the audit junior definitely refer to their supervisor?

		✔
(a)	An invoice for 'consultancy fees' addressed to the Managing Director and posted to 'raw materials purchases'	
(b)	A purchase invoice for a motor vehicle posted to 'Non-current assets – Vehicles'	
(c)	A material purchase invoice for stock not checked and not supported by an order or delivery note	
(d)	A material purchases invoice for legal fees	

Task 22

ISA 265 *Communicating significant deficiencies in internal control* defines a significant deficiency in internal control as a deficiency or combination of deficiencies that, in the auditors' professional judgement, is of sufficient importance to merit the attention of those charged with governance.

Identify whether the following deficiency in interal control is a significant deficiency.

The client carries out monthly bank reconciliations for all its bank accounts. A review by the auditors of these revealed that, contrary to company policy, two of them had not been formally signed by the Finance Director.

Significant / Not significant

Task 23

During the audit of the purchases system at Whoppa Ltd, a manufacturer of double glazed windows and doors, the audit team identifies that there are no procedures for approving suppliers and that purchase orders are always sent to the same few suppliers.

Whoppa Ltd has used the same suppliers for many years and the audit team is told that they have a good relationship with them. The client says that these are regular suppliers who know Whoppa Ltd's requirements and that they are reliable and provide goods of the right quality. The Purchasing Assistant believes that formally approving suppliers is a waste of time as they would end up selecting the same suppliers. She therefore does not see the point of doing it.

Prepare extracts, suitable for inclusion in a report to the management of Whoppa Ltd, which set out:

(1)   the possible consequences of these two problem areas and

(2)   the recommendations that you would make in respect of each point.

It is suggested that you set out your answer in the form of a table.

Problem areas	Consequences	Recommendations
The company does not have any procedures for approving suppliers		
Purchase orders are always sent to the same few suppliers		

Task 24

Auditors use tests of control and substantive procedures to gather audit evidence.

For each of the procedures listed below, select whether it is a test of control or a substantive procedure.

	Test of control	Substantive procedure
(a) Reperformance of the bank reconciliation at the date of the Statement of Financial Position		
(b) Comparison of the current year's results with last year and with the budget for the current year		
(c) Check for authorisation of overtime payments		

Task 25

You are reviewing the files following completion of the audit work on three audit clients and find that the audit files contain the following points.

In each instance indicate how the problems identified might affect the Audit Report.

Bing Ltd

The audit team was unable to physically inspect vehicles and equipment to the value of £3.2m as part of non-current assets with a total value of £5m as they were located throughout the country. The audit team were unable to check whether individual items were insured as no details of individual assets were given. Vehicle log books were inspected for all vehicles. Purchase invoices had been seen for all additions and sales invoices for all disposals. The asset register was reconciled to the nominal ledger.

✔

(a) Not modified	
Modified:	
(b) 'Except for' – limitation of scope	
(c) 'Except for' – material disagreement	
(d) Disclaimer – pervasive limitation of scope	
(e) Adverse opinion – pervasive disagreement	

Bong Ltd

You are auditing the financial statements which have been prepared in the same way as those of previous periods. You discover that the company had recently defaulted on its quarterly loan instalment which was due one month after the year-end. They attributed this to a 'financing error' and made the required repayment two weeks later than they should have done. You discover that to make the payment Bong Ltd has taken out a short-term loan from another company owned by the Managing Director's brother. Bong Ltd has been at the limit of its overdraft facilities throughout the financial period and the repayment of the loan to the Managing Director's brother together with another quarterly loan repayment is due in two months. You discover that the bank has written to Bong Ltd stating that if the repayment is late this time they will be demanding the repayment of the whole loan amount immediately. If this happens, it is obvious that they would not be able to do this.

✔

(a) Not modified	
Modified:	
(b) 'Except for' – limitation of scope	
(c) 'Except for' – material disagreement	
(d) Disclaimer – pervasive limitation of scope	
(e) Adverse opinion – pervasive disagreement	

Bang Ltd

Your firm has been appointed auditors of Bang Ltd three months after its year-end as Bang Ltd's previous audit firm resigned. The company is a manufacturer and distributor of electrical components. It has a very efficient internal audit department and your audit work on its systems reveals no major weaknesses except for some internal control weaknesses in the purchasing system, none of which are of major significance. You carry out substantive testing on items in the Statement of Financial Position and these also give no cause for concern. You are unable to verify the existence of some of the non-current assets in the Statement of Financial Position as they were sold after the year-end.

	✔
(a) Not modified	
Modified:	
(b) 'Except for' – limitation of scope	
(c) 'Except for' – material disagreement	
(d) Disclaimer – pervasive limitation of scope	
(e) Adverse opinion – pervasive disagreement	

Task 26

During the course of the audit of Mungo Ltd, a construction company, you discover that the company may be paying bribes in order to obtain work. Your evidence is based on various unexplained 'round sum' cash payments which have been included as 'site costs' in the nominal ledger. Some of these payments amount to several thousand pounds and there does not appear to be any documentation to support the amounts paid. There does not appear to be any commercial reason why such substantial cash payments are being made.

When you questioned the management and staff you were told that the Sales Director was responsible for making these payments and has all the relevant paperwork as these items were confidential. The Sales Director is proving difficult to track down and is constantly avoiding the auditors.

In this situation, decide which course of action you should take.   ✔

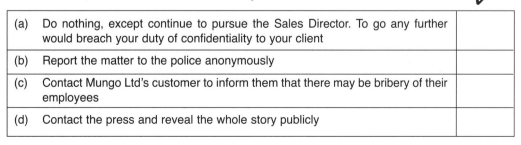

(a)	Do nothing, except continue to pursue the Sales Director. To go any further would breach your duty of confidentiality to your client	
(b)	Report the matter to the police anonymously	
(c)	Contact Mungo Ltd's customer to inform them that there may be bribery of their employees	
(d)	Contact the press and reveal the whole story publicly	

Choose **one** option.

Task 27

An audit benefits a company because it:

               ✔

(a)	Reassures the shareholders that the financial statements are accurate	
(b)	Makes the management accountable to the shareholders	
(c)	Guarantees that the accounts are free from fraud or error	
(d)	Guarantees that the financial information shown is true and fair	

Choose **one** option.

Task 28

State whether the following statements are true or false.

               ✔

		True	False
(a)	Auditors can limit their liability under a claim by a client for negligence by agreement with the directors		
(b)	Audit firms are allowed to operate as limited liability companies		

Task 29

The role of the Financial Reporting Council does not include:

               ✔

(a)	Establishing high standards of auditing	
(b)	Meeting the developing needs of users of financial information	
(c)	Ensuring public confidence in the auditing process	
(d)	Issuing International Accounting Standards	

Choose **one** option.

Task 30

The external auditor assesses control risk in order to determine the audit approach.

Select whether the following factors are likely to lead to the auditor assessing that there is an increase or decrease in control risk.

	Increase	Decrease
(a) A new company accountant has been appointed who is not qualified		
(b) In order to reduce costs the management has decided to make two members of staff redundant from the accounts department		
(c) A new computerised accounting system has been installed but to date the staff training programme for this system has not been completed		

Task 31

Which of the following statements best describes the auditors approach to materiality?

Choose **one** option.

(a)	The level of materiality is a matter for professional judgement	
(b)	Materiality is set at the planning stage and is not changed during the audit	
(c)	Materiality is based on the size of errors or misstatements the auditors will accept as reasonable	
(d)	Materiality limits are based on both the financial statements from previous years and the level of tolerable errors the auditors will accept in the current period	

Task 32

One of the ways of obtaining sufficient reliable audit evidence is through questioning client's staff either informally or at formal meetings. The types of questions asked can be Open, Closed or Reflective.

Identify whether each of these is an Open, Closed or Reflective question.

✔

		Open	**Closed**	**Reflective**
(a)	How does the company know that the only individuals being paid are current employees?			
(b)	Does Mrs Jones have total responsibility for credit control?			
(c)	Do you think that the inventory system can detect when goods are being stolen by staff?			

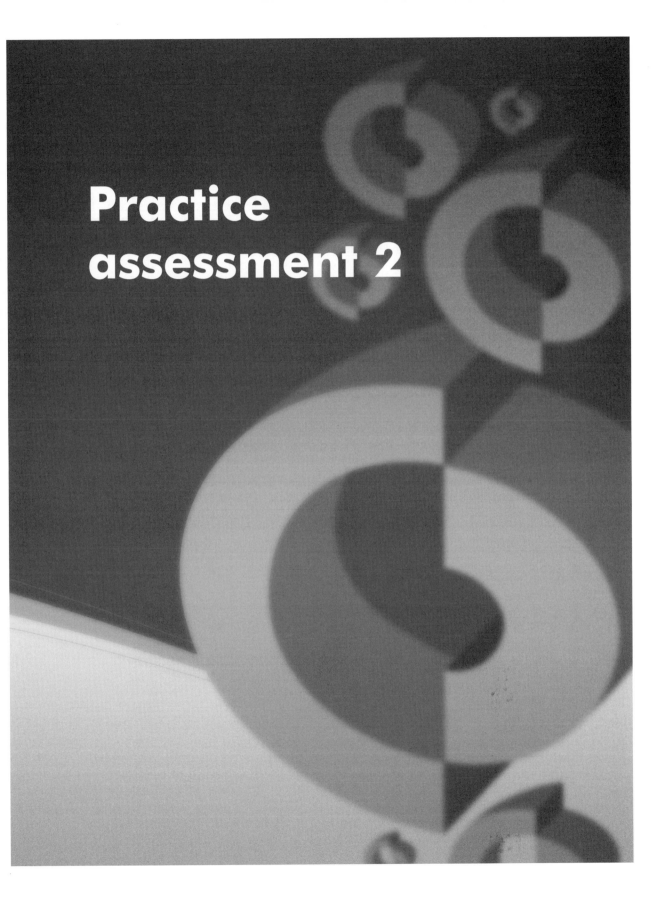

Practice assessment 2

Task 1

Auditors must obtain an understanding of a client's control environment and must assess the strength of these controls in order to decide whether or not they can rely on them.

Select whether the following factors contribute to a strong control environment, a weak control environment, or have no effect.

✔

	Strong	Weak	No effect
(a) The client has an independent internal audit department			
(b) The client has only a small administrative section and most of the accounts work is handled by three people who do not have fixed roles. They carry out each task depending on who is available when it needs to be done			

Task 2

Accounting systems have control objectives and control procedures to minimise the risk that the control objective is not met.

Identify whether the following is a risk, control objective or control procedure by ticking the appropriate box.

✔

	Risk	Control objective	Control procedure
(a) Customers may refuse to pay for goods if there is no proof of delivery			
(b) All overtime worked has to be authorised by a manager			
(c) The company only pays for goods which have been delivered and are fit for purpose			

Task 3

The external auditor may seek to place reliance on internal controls in order to restrict substantive testing.

In each of the following circumstances, select whether the external auditor is likely to place reliance or place no reliance on internal controls.

✔

	Reliance	No reliance
(a) A company where the processing of accounting transactions is undertaken by one person		
(b) A company which has an internal audit function which monitors operational and financial controls		
(c) A company which has internal controls with a history of management override		

Task 4

Auditors are required to give either limited or reasonable assurance.

Which of these assignments would be one where reasonable assurance is required?

Select **one** answer.

✔

(a)	Assignment to certify an application for a government grant	
(b)	Assignment to review the books of a possible takeover company	
(c)	Assignments to carry out the first audit of a new company on behalf of shareholders	
(d)	Assignment to carry out an internal audit review of the purchasing inventory system	

Task 5

External auditors use a variety of methods for documenting systems of control, including flowcharts, internal control questionnaires and internal control checklists.

For each of the following descriptions select whether it represents a flowchart, internal control questionnaire or internal control checklist.

✔

	Flowchart	Questionnaire	Checklist
(a) A listing of controls necessary to provide reasonable assurance of effective internal control within a given transaction cycle			
(b) A pictorial presentation of the processing steps within a given transaction cycle			

Task 6

When planning an audit of financial statements, the external auditor is required to consider how factors such as the entity's operating environment and its system of internal control affect the risk of misstatement in the financial statements.

Select whether the following factors are likely to increase, reduce, or have no effect on the risk of misstatement.

✔

	Increase	Reduce	No effect
(a) The entity is committed to employing personnel with appropriate accounting and financial reporting skills			
(b) The entity is to be sold and the purchase consideration will be determined as a multiple of reported profit			
(c) The entity's management does not intend to remedy deficiencies in internal controls identified by the external auditor			

Task 7

For each of the following control procedures decide which of the risks will be addressed:

✔

Control procedure	Risk of non-payment for goods	Risk of failing to process customer orders	Poor cash management
(a) An aged trade receivables analysis is produced at the end of each month. Customers with overdue balances are sent a reminder letter			
(b) All customer orders are recorded on pre-numbered order pads and signed by the person taking the order			
(c) The delivery driver must obtain a signature on the delivery note from all customers. This delivery note must be passed to the accounts department			

Task 8

The following are examples of procedures carried out by an audit client, Sploshers Ltd, a manufacturer of soft drinks.

Identify whether each procedure is a strength or a significant weakness by selecting the appropriate option.

✔

	Strength	Significant weakness
(a) The company counts the inventory of bulk raw materials at the end of each month but does not count finished products at all as they believe there is always movement in and out which would make it difficult. Inventory of finished product makes up about 40% of the total inventory valuation		
(b) At the end of each month the Financial Controller reconciles the balances on all bank accounts and formally documents the bank reconciliations		
(c) The directors hold a monthly meeting at which they review Sploshers Ltd's actual performance for the month against budget. They investigate any significant differences		

Task 9

An audit client, Sploshers Ltd, carries out an analytical review on the revenue and purchases elements of its monthly management accounts.

During the last financial year the company had to make certain changes to the way in which it carried out business. Some of these changes resulted in significant differences in its analysis of revenue and purchases.

For each of the following changes decide whether it would be likely to have a significant effect on Sploshers Ltd's analysis of revenue and purchases.

	Effect	No effect
(a) Selling prices of all products were reduced by an average of 8% in a bid to gain market share		
(b) Sploshers Ltd carried out a review of all its suppliers and renegotiated supply contracts to include longer credit terms		
(c) Sploshers Ltd reviewed its banking policies and moved some of its bank accounts to a new bank which offered lower bank charges and a lower rate of interest on borrowings		

Task 10

The objective of a substantive test will determine the population from which the sample for testing is selected.

For each of the objectives set out below, select the population from which the sample should be selected.

(a) Obtain evidence of the existence of a non-current asset

> **Non-current asset register / Physical asset**

(b) Obtain evidence of the completeness of the trade payables balance

> **Purchase ledger entries / Goods received records**

Task 11

Auditors use tests of control and substantive procedures to gather audit evidence.

For each of the procedures listed below, select whether it is a test of control or a substantive procedure.

	Test of control	Substantive procedure
(a) Comparison of the current year's revenue figure with the previous year's figure		
(b) Observation of the despatch procedures in respect of goods leaving an entity's warehouse		
(c) Vouching of an addition to non-current assets to the supplier's invoice		

Task 12

You are the audit manager and are currently reviewing the audit programme for Receivables.

The audit objective is to verify the total amount of Receivables shown in the Statement of Financial Position.

From the list below decide which **two** tests will be most effective in meeting this objective.

(a)	Compare total Receivables with the total for the previous year	
(b)	Carry out an aged analysis of Receivables balances and review any balances outstanding for more than 60 days	
(c)	Carry out an analytical review on the Receivables balances to calculate the average trade receivables collection period	
(d)	Vouch a selection of sales invoices to the Receivables ledger	

Task 13

During the year ended 31 December 20X9, Becks Ltd took out a bank loan of £1 million to fund a capital project. The terms of the loan require:

· Capital repayments, over 5 years, in monthly instalments commencing 1 July 20X9

· Interest at 9% per annum payable monthly

· Profit before interest and tax in the monthly management accounts to cover interest at least four times

Set out, in a manner suitable for inclusion in the audit plan:

(1) The audit risks relating to the loan; and

(2) The procedures to be undertaken in order to ensure that the loan is properly classified and disclosed in the financial statements.

Task 14

As part of their testing to verify revenues, an auditor will inspect purchase invoices. The auditor will gain assurance about different assertions depending on the information included in the invoice.

For each piece of the information below, select **one** assertion for which it will provide assurance.

✔

	Accuracy	Classification	Cut-off	Existence
(a) Date of the invoice				
(b) Description of the item purchased				
(c) Monetary amount				

Task 15

Two types of computer-assisted audit techniques (CAAT) are test data and audit software.

For each of the procedures listed below, select the type of CAAT which would be used to perform that procedure.

✔

	Test data	Audit software
(a) Comparison of the cost and net realisable value of inventory items to determine the lower value		
(b) Input of data with false inventory code numbers to check that the system rejects such data		
(c) Extraction of inventory balances over £5,000 in order to carry out further testing		

Task 16

The auditor is responsible for gathering sufficient reliable evidence to ensure that the financial statements are free from significant misstatements.

Preliminary discussions with management during the planning phase of an audit has revealed three items of information which may or may not lead to an increased risk of a significant misstatement arising.

Indicate whether each of the following is likely to increase or reduce the risk of a significant misstatement.

✔

	Increase risk of misstatement	Reduce risk of misstatement
(a) The company has formed a joint venture with a partnership based in a tax haven		
(b) The company has appointed three new non executive directors to the Board who have formed an Audit Committee		
(c) The executive directors have been granted very large share options whereby they can buy shares cheaply and sell them at the market price after a period of time		

Task 17

The following are descriptions of procedures within the payroll system of Delaware Ltd.

For each procedure, select whether it is a strength or a weakness.

✔

	Strength	Weakness
(a) The computerised payroll is processed weekly by Amelia who is also responsible for amending the standing data details such as the addition of new employees and changes to wage rates		
(b) The managing director, David Delaware, reviews the BACS listing of net pay details per employee and signs the listing before authorising the assistant accountant, Marie, to transmit the details to the company's bank		

Task 18

Select whether the following statements, in respect of an external auditor's working papers, are true or false.

✔

		True	False
(a)	Working papers are prepared by the external auditor because there is a legal requirement to do so		
(b)	The objective of working papers is to provide evidence that the audit was planned and performed in accordance with International Standards on Auditing		
(c)	Working papers should contain the name of who performed the audit work and the date it was performed		

Task 19

You are part of an external audit team. During the final review of the financial statements you discover a note on the audit file. It says that a change in legislation will mean that the client must repackage a substantial amount of its finished goods inventory in order to comply with the new legislation. The cost of this repackaging has been estimated at £40,000. If the goods are not repackaged they will have no value as they cannot be sold in their current state.

The value of the finished goods inventory affected is £375,000. Total inventory is £850,000. Materiality has been set at £50,000.

Identify whether or not the inventory valuation needs to be adjusted so that an unmodified audit opinion can be issued.

(a)	The value of finished goods inventory is overstated and should be amended	
(b)	The adjustment is not material so the value of finished goods inventory does not need to be adjusted	

Task 20

Engco Ltd is a company which undertakes industrial maintenance services under short-term fixed-price contracts. All direct costs (labour and materials) relating to each contract are recorded in the company's job costing system which is integrated with the purchases and payroll applications. The job costing records are used by the finance director to estimate the value of work in progress for the monthly management accounts and the year-end financial statements. For the work in progress valuation, a percentage is added to the direct costs to cover overheads. The finance director determines the percentage by taking the production overheads figure in the management accounts as a percentage of direct costs in the management accounts.

Set out, in a manner suitable for inclusion in the audit plan, the audit procedures to be undertaken in order to ensure that work in progress is fairly stated in the financial statements.

Task 21

During the external audit of Pike Ltd, the audit junior identified two instances of failure to authorise purchase invoices prior to posting to the purchase ledger. Both instances occurred when the purchase supervisor who is responsible for authorising such transactions was away on sick leave, and further tests indicated no similar failings following her return to work.

In respect of this matter, select whether the audit junior should take no further action or refer to the supervisor.

No further action / Refer to supervisor

Task 22

During the external audit of Beech Ltd, the audit junior identified an invoice for the cost of school fees for the managing director's children. The purchase ledger clerk informed the audit junior that the managing director had told her to hide the costs in sundries. The amount of the school fees is insignificant in terms of key figures in the financial statements.

In respect of this matter, select whether the audit junior should take no further action or refer to the supervisor.

No further action / Refer to supervisor

Task 23

During the audit of Media Ltd, a film production company, it was discovered that although the company maintained a non-current asset register to record the details of its cameras and other equipment, no checking procedures other than reconciliation with the nominal ledger are undertaken.

Prepare extracts, suitable for inclusion in a report to management of Media Ltd, which set out

(1)   the possible consequences of this

(2)   the recommendations that you would make in respect of this matter.

Task 24

The external auditor has a duty to report to management any significant deficiencies arising during the course of the audit.

If the deficiencies are of such significance that they might affect the financial decisions of a reader of the financial statements the auditors may have to consider modifying their audit report.

Identify whether the following deficiency, taken in isolation, will cause the auditor to report the deficiency to management only or modify their auditor's report only:

A long term contract to construct a brand new marina has run into serious delays and, as a consequence, a provision for losses on the contract must be made in the client's financial statements. This was overlooked when the financial statements were first prepared due the costing department having failed to revise the costing schedule for the marina contract. The directors have agreed to amend the financial statements as the amount involved is material.

		✔
(a)	Modify auditor's report only	
(b)	Include in report to management only	

Task 25

The error listed below has been detected during the audit of Taurus Ltd. The directors of Taurus refuse to make an adjustment to correct the error.

The audit firm Able Kahn LLP uses 5% of profit before tax as the yardstick to determine whether errors are material. Taurus Ltd's profit before tax is £100,000.

Select whether or not the following error requires to be adjusted in order to issue an unmodified audit opinion on the financial statements:

An overstatement of inventory amounting to £4,200, and an overstatement of receivables amounting to £3,800.

Requires to be adjusted / Does not require to be adjusted

Task 26

As part of the audit of Puffers plc you are reviewing the purchasing system.

You discover that the Purchasing Manager has formed his own company called Buynow Ltd and that Puffers plc purchases much of its raw materials and equipment from this company. The amounts involved are significant.

Orders for Buynow Ltd are approved by the Purchasing Manager, only and he arranges for the outstanding balance at the end of each month to be paid promptly, before other suppliers.

You carry out a search on Buynow Ltd at Companies House and discover that one of the other directors is the wife of the Technical Director of Puffers plc.

In this situation what initial action should you take? Select the appropriate option from the list below.

	✔
(a) This is a fraud – inform the police without discussion with the directors of Puffers plc	
(b) Report the fraud to the directors of Puffers plc and then inform the police	
(c) Report the fraud to the directors of Puffers plc and await their response	

Task 27

Complete the following extract from ISA 240 '*The auditor's responsibility relating to fraud in an audit of financial statements*' by selecting the appropriate words from the list below.

'The objectives of the auditor are:

(a)   To identify and . . . . the risks of . . . . misstatement of the

financial statements due to fraud;

(b)   To obtain sufficient . . . . audit evidence regarding the assessed risks of

material misstatement due to fraud, through designing and implementing appropriate

responses.'

- assess
- judge
- overall
- significant
- material
- appropriate
- proper

Task 28

State whether the following statements are true or false in respect of external auditors' liability.

	True	False
(a) External auditors are liable to anybody who relies solely on the audit report on financial statements when making investment decisions		
(b) External auditors may limit their liability to third parties if they include a disclaimer of liability in their audit report		

Task 29

Which one of the following best describes the role of the International Auditing and Assurance Board (IAASB)?

The IAASB is responsible for:

(a)	Setting auditing standards which are compulsory throughout the world	
(b)	Monitoring auditors to ensure that they comply with auditing standards	
(c)	Investigating and disciplining auditors who fail to comply with auditing standards	
(d)	Setting auditing standards which facilitate the convergence of national and international auditing standards	

Task 30

The external auditor assesses control risk in order to determine the audit approach.

Select whether the following factors are likely to lead to the auditor assessing that there is an increase or decrease in control risk.

	Increase	Decrease
(a) The allocation of responsibilities so that different personnel are responsible for the authorisation, processing and recording of transactions		
(b) Management has a positive attitude and discipline towards controls and their enforcement		
(c) The accounting staff are inexperienced and have a poor understanding of accounting principles		

Task 31

Select whether the following statements in respect of performance materiality are true or false.

	True	False
(a) Performance materiality should be set at a level below the level of materiality for the financial statements as a whole		
(b) Once established, performance materiality must not be changed as the audit progresses		

Task 32

One of the ways of obtaining sufficient reliable audit evidence is through questioning client's staff either informally or at formal meetings. The types of questions asked can be Open, Closed or Reflective.

Identify whether each of these is an Open, Closed or reflective question.

	Open	Closed	Reflective
(a) Bank reconciliations are carried out every month, aren't they?			
(b) What is the system for identifying obsolete inventory?			
(c) You said there had been some trouble with the computer system – how serious was the problem?			

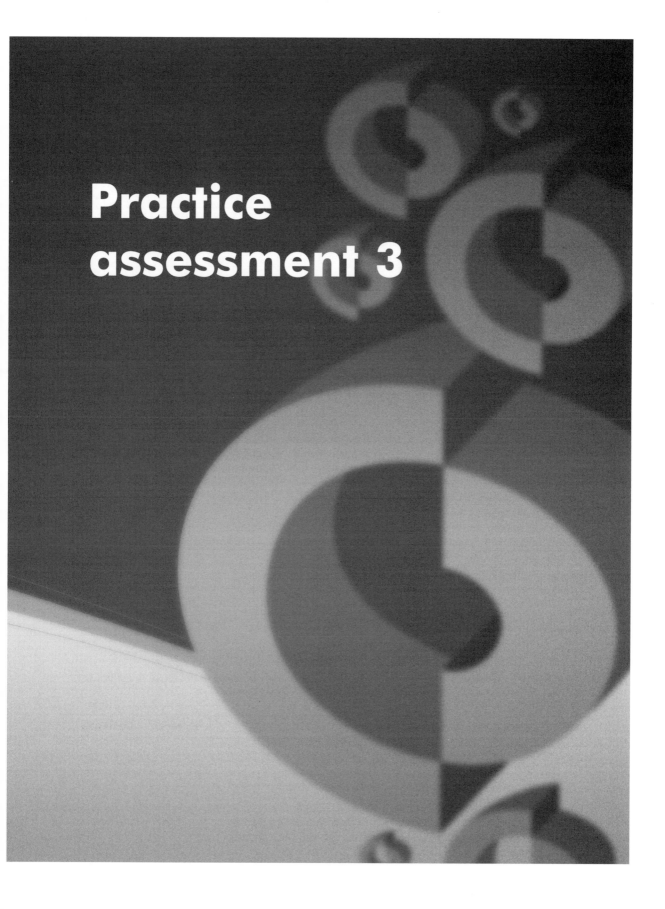

Practice assessment 3

Task 1

Auditors must obtain an understanding of a client's control environment and must assess the strength of these controls in order to decide whether or not they can rely on them.

Identify whether each of the following statements regarding an auditor's reliance on internal controls is true or false by selecting the correct option.

✔

	True	False
(a) Auditors can always rely on the client's internal controls if the client has an internal audit department		
(b) Auditors must gather sufficient reliable evidence to enable them to decide whether to rely on client's internal controls		
(c) Auditors should never rely on internal controls alone and in all cases should carry out significant substantive testing		

Task 2

For each of the following control procedures decide which of the risks will be addressed.

✔

Control procedure	Risk of paying for goods not ordered	Risk of ordering excessive amounts of goods	Risk of running out of goods for resale
(a) All purchase orders must be authorised by the Purchasing Manager			
(b) All purchases to be ordered by the purchasing department			

Task 3

For each of the following factors identify whether there is an increase or decrease in control risk.

✔

	Increase	Decrease
(a) The audit client has recently installed a computerised inventory control system		
(b) The audit client has recently made three members of staff redundant from the accounts department		
(c) The audit client has outsourced cash collection procedures at all its supermarket branches to an external security company		

Task 4

Auditors are required to give either limited or reasonable assurance.

Which of these assignments would be one where reasonable assurance is required?

		✔
(a)	Carry out a fraud investigation	
(b)	Carry out a review of the client's internal controls and recommend improvements	
(c)	Prepare budgets and forecasts for a client to support an application for additional bank finance	
(d)	None of the above	

Task 5

The external auditor of Bubbles Ltd has used an Internal Control Questionnaire to assist in the evaluation of the internal controls of the company's purchasing system.

Below are some of the questions and responses. Identify whether the answers to the questions indicate a control or lack of control.

		Control	Lack of control
(a)	Do all purchase orders have to be authorised by the purchasing manager? Answer NO		
(b)	Do all purchases have to be made from approved suppliers? Answer YES		
(c)	Are all supplier invoices received checked against purchase orders and goods received notes? Answer NO – goods received notes only		

Task 6

Identify for each of the following factors whether there is an increase or decrease in control risk.

		Increase	Decrease
(a)	The audited entity has an internal audit department which reports to the Finance Director		
(b)	The audited entity has recently installed a new management information system		
(c)	The audited entity has instituted a new procedure where all overtime claims must be authorised by the Factory Manager		

Task 7

An entity uses internal controls to reduce the risk of error or misstatement.

Identify from the list below the risk mitigated by the appropriate procedure in connection with payroll and petty cash procedures.

Internal control procedure	Risk mitigated
(a) Obtaining new employee's details is the responsibility of the Human Resources Department which then forwards them to the Payroll Department so that the employee can be included in the payroll	
(b) All payments from petty cash must be supported by an authorised petty cash voucher	
(c) Commission paid to sales staff must be agreed by the Sales Manager and can only be claimed when the customer has actually paid for the sales to which the commission relates	

(1)   Risk of fictitious employees being included on the payroll

(2)   Theft

(3)   Risk of errors when the Payroll Department is setting up the employee master files

(4)   Risk of payment for work not done

(5)   Risk of commission being paid on false or fictitious sales

Task 8

The following are descriptions of procedures within Exodus Ltd. Identify whether each of the following procedures is a strength or a weakness by selecting the appropriate option.

✔

	Strength	Weakness
(a) The sale of scrap and waste material is carried out by the Warehouse Manager		
(b) Goods received notes are prepared for all items delivered to the Goods Inwards Department		

Task 9

The external auditor is required to undertake analytical procedures as part of the planning process to identify movements out of line with expectation.

The trade receivables collection period of Oxberry Ltd for the year ended 30 June 20X2 is 34 days compared to 44 days for the year ended 30 June 20X1.

Which **two** of the following may provide a reasonable explanation for the fall in Oxberry Ltd's trade receivables collection period?

✔

(a) Invoices relating to sales made in June 20X2 were posted to the ledger accounts in July 20X2	
(b) Invoices relating to sales made in July 20X2 were posted to the ledger accounts in June 20X2	
(c) Oxberry Ltd have extended the credit terms available to its customers	
(d) Oxberry Ltd have tightened the credit terms available to its customers	

Task 10

When selecting items in order to perform tests of detail, the auditor has to consider a number of factors.

For each of the following factors, select whether they will result in an increase or a decrease in sample size.

✔

	Increase	Decrease
(a) An increase in the auditor's assessment of risk of misstatement		
(b) An increase in the use of other substantive procedures directed at the same assertion		
(c) Stratification of the population being tested		

Task 11

Auditors carry out a mixture of compliance and substantive testing during the course of their audit work.

Decide whether each of the following statements is true or false.

	True	False ✔
(a) Substantive testing of trade payables balances should be carried out when all balances are material		
(b) Value weighted selection (monetary unit sampling) is a good way of testing for overstatement of balances		

Task 12

Decide which of the following is **not** an appropriate test for auditing Payroll.

	✔
(a) Review a sample of new starters in the year to ensure they have been correctly added to the payroll system in the appropriate month	
(b) Re-perform calculations of gross pay and deductions from pay for a sample of employees	
(c) Ask the Company Accountant to confirm the existence of all employees on the payroll	
(d) For a sample of employees throughout the year, confirm net payment made to the BACS summary	

Task 13

You are planning the audit of Missing Ltd a construction company. During the planning phase you have been told that the company has constructed a major extension to its factory and a new office block to house the research and development department.

Missing Ltd constructed the buildings using its own labour and resources. A separate cost account was set up for the project and the company charged to this account all the materials used, the cost of labour at Missing Ltd's standard charge-out rate and an overhead cost based on the number of hours worked. The balance on this account has been included in non-current assets as part of the cost of buildings.

Identify and explain the audit risks attached to the valuation of these non-current assets and where there may be a specific risk of misstatement.

Task 14

Which of the following is **not** an appropriate test for auditing the trade receivables balance at the year end?

		✔
(a)	A trade receivables circularisation	
(b)	A review of receipts from customers after the year-end	
(c)	Testing cut-off procedures for deliveries made to customers around the year end	
(d)	Performing a walk through test of the revenue system	

Task 15

Auditors are increasingly using Computer Assisted Auditing Techniques (CAATs) as part of their audit testing.

Identify whether the following statements are true or false.

		True	False
(a)	Audit interrogation software can be used to generate exception reports showing unusual transactions		
(b)	Audit software is expensive and can only be used by computer experts to detect fraudulent transactions		

Task 16

The auditor is responsible for gathering sufficient reliable evidence to ensure that the financial statements are free from significant misstatements.

Preliminary discussions with management during the planning phase of an audit has revealed three items of information which may or may not lead to an increased risk of a significant misstatement arising.

Indicate whether each of the following is likely to increase or reduce the risk of a significant misstatement.

	Increase risk of misstatement	Reduce risk of misstatement
(a) Part of the financial records were lost when a computer error meant that all the accounting records for two weeks in December were lost		
(b) The head of the internal audit department has left the organisation and will not be replaced. It has been decided that the Financial Director will head up the department going forward		
(c) The company has recently introduced computer assisted auditing techniques (CAATs) into its computerised accounting system which monitor transaction parameters and operator activity		

Task 17

Answers to an Internal Control Questionnaire (ICQ) for Poppet Ltd indicate that procedures are in place to authorise the payment of staff for overtime worked.

Indicate whether or not this would provide assurance on each of the following control objectives.

	Provides assurance	Does not provide assurance
(a) Employees are only being paid for work done		
(b) Employees are being paid at the correct hourly rate		

Task 18

Select whether the following statements in respect of an external auditors' working papers are true or false.

✔

	True	False
(a) The auditor must substantiate their audit opinion by demonstrating that they have gathered sufficient reliable evidence to support it		
(b) Working papers should clearly identify who carried out the appropriate audit work. This is primarily so that blame can be allocated if it is later found that mistakes have been made		
(c) Permanent audit files contain the client details which do not change significantly from year to year. For example, details of the company's constitution, names of its lawyers and bankers and documentation of its internal procedures		

Task 19

For each of the following audit points decide what action the audit junior should take.

Select **one** option for each issue.

✔

	Refer to Audit Supervisor	Take no further action
(a) The bank reconciliation for August was not carried out as the client's accountant was on holiday. The reconciliation carried out for September showed no outstanding issues		
(b) The count sheets completed by client's staff at the year-end inventory count have been accidentally shredded by the office junior		
(c) A test of a sample of trade receivables balances revealed that 7 out of the 20 balances tested exceeded the customer's credit limit		
(d) When looking at petty cash no receipts could be found for purchases of milk for the accounts office amounting to approximately £5 per week		
(e) When testing purchase orders out of a sample of 40, 8 had not been properly authorised		

Task 20

As part of its non-current assets an entity may include on its Statement of Financial Position a number of intangible assets, in particular, goodwill, patents and trade marks and copyright.

Indicate the audit procedures required to verify the assertions relating to intangible assets in particular, existence, ownership, completeness and valuation.

Task 21

Which **two** of these sales invoices should the audit junior immediately refer to their supervisor?

✔

(a)	An invoice for the sale of used equipment posted to non-current asset sales account	
(b)	An invoice for 'Consultancy Advice' addressed to a company based in Panama	
(c)	A material invoice for a sale of goods addressed to a major customer which was cancelled and a credit note immediately after the year-end	
(d)	An invoice for the sale of goods addressed to the Finance Director showing a 50% discount on normal prices	

Task 22

ISA 265 *Communicating significant deficiencies in internal control* defines a significant deficiency in internal control as a deficiency or combination of deficiencies that, in the auditor's professional judgement, is of sufficient importance to merit the attention of those charged with governance.

Identify whether the following deficiency in internal control is a significant deficiency.

Audit work revealed that there were no controls over the disposal of scrap raw materials and damaged products. The storekeepers disposed of these items.

> **Significant / Not significant**

Task 23

The firm that you work for has just taken over as the auditors of Piggles Ltd a wholesaler of motor vehicle parts. While reviewing the client's accounting systems you discover that the purchasing system is controlled by two members of staff who:

- place telephone orders with suppliers for new inventory whenever the Warehouse Manager tells them a particular item is running low
- negotiate prices and discounts with suppliers
- match supplier invoices with delivery notes from the warehouse
- enter invoices into the purchases ledger
- make payments to suppliers as they feel appropriate – any supplier statements received are not retained
- record the payments made in the purchases ledger
- obtain credit notes for damaged or faulty goods on the basis of information provided by the Warehouse Manager

The individuals concerned have been working at Piggles Ltd for many years and share the work between them with no specific individual responsibilities.

Prepare extracts suitable for inclusion in a report to the management of Piggles Ltd indicating the possible consequences of these arrangements and your recommendations for improvement.

Task 24

ISA 265 *Communicating deficiencies in internal control to those charged with governance and management* defines a significant deficiency in internal control as 'a deficiency or combination of deficiencies that, in the auditor's professional judgement is of sufficient importance to merit the attention of those charged with governance.'

Decide whether the following deficiency in internal control is a significant deficiency.

The audit of cash payments revealed that the company employed a number of casual workers for part of the year who were paid in cash.

Significant / Not significant

Task 25

The computer system of an audit client, Tweetiepie Ltd, was damaged by a fire in the company's offices. Consequently the financial records for one month of the year were lost. The accounting records have now been recovered from the computer backups but all supporting documentation was permanently destroyed. The directors of Tweetiepie Ltd believe that the financial statements are correctly stated and the auditors do not disagree with this.

In this situation decide what type of audit opinion should be given.

Modified opinion / Unmodified opinion

Task 26

Your firm acts as auditor to DishDash Ltd a firm run by two brothers.

Each brother contacts you stating that they have had a huge disagreement and can no longer work together. They wish to split up the business. Each of them ask you to work with him to advise him in the dispute and in setting up a new business.

Decide whether the following is appropriate action to take in this situation.

Act for both brothers but take care not to reveal any information about one brother's activities to the other.

Appropriate / Not appropriate

Task 27

Identify whether each of the following statements is an objective of the management of an organisation or an objective of an external auditor.

✔

		Management objective	External audit objective
(a)	Correct calculation of corporation tax liabilities based on the profit for the financial year		
(b)	Confirmation that the accounts have been prepared under the historical cost convention		
(c)	Filing of annual financial statements with the Registrar of Companies		

Task 28

Auditors have a responsibility to shareholders. They also have a duty of care to third parties which arises where the auditors are aware that the financial statements they are auditing may be relied upon by a third party.

There are various steps that auditors can take to limit their liability for claims made by third parties. Which of the following steps might **not** serve to limit the effect of a successful claim against the auditors for negligence?

✔

(a)	Operating as a limited liability partnership	
(b)	Taking out professional indemnity insurance	
(c)	Including the Bannerman wording in the audit report	
(d)	Entering into a limited liability agreement with shareholders	

Task 29

Which **one** of the following statements on International standards on Auditing ISAs is true?

✔

(a)	ISAs apply to both internal and external auditors	
(b)	Auditors are permitted to deviate from the requirements of ISAs in exceptional circumstances provided they can justify their actions	
(c)	ISAs are applied to both budgeted and forecasted financial information and also to historical financial information	

Task 30

Decide whether each of the following changes will increase or reduce audit risk.

Select **one** option for each change.

	Increase audit risk	Reduce audit risk
(a) An audit client has recently merged with another organisation that is audited by another audit firm. Your firm has taken over the whole audit.		
(b) An audit client has recently set up an audit committee of non-executive directors. The Internal Audit department will now report to the audit committee.		

Task 31

Materiality can be defined as being an error or misstatement which could reasonably be expected to influence the economic decisions of a user of the financial statements.

Decide whether each of the following errors identified during the course of an audit are likely to be considered material.

	Material	Not material
(a) An error in the valuation of inventory of £100,000. Pre-tax profits are £1.9m		
(b) The wife of the Managing Director is providing legal services to the company. This is not disclosed in the financial statements		
(c) An error of £2m in the depreciation of non-current assets. The net asset value of the business is £50m and profit for the year is £62m		
(d) A loss on a contract in progress to build a dam in Zambia. The loss is expected to be £20m. The profit for the year is £80m and the net asset value is £700m		

Task 32

One of the ways of obtaining sufficient reliable audit evidence is through questioning client's staff either informally or at formal meetings. The types of questions asked can be open, closed or reflective.

Identify whether each of the following questions is open, closed or reflective.

✔

	Open	Closed	Reflective
(a) The new Finance Director has certainly made a difference hasn't she?			
(b) When you said that the staff in the stores had their own way of doing things what did you mean by that?			
(c) Will the upgrade to the computerised accounting system make things easier?			
(d) What do you think the chances are of buying the new warehouse before the year-end?			

Practice assessment 1 answers

Task 1

(b) No one person has complete control of any aspect of the accounting function

Task 2

ALL procedures would be considered as **weaknesses**.

Task 3

(a) Reliance; (b) and (c) No reliance

Task 4

(d) None of the above

Task 5

(a) and (c) Flowchart; (b) ICQ

Task 6

(a) and (b) Weak; (c) Strong; (d) No effect

Task 7

(a) Risk; (b) Control objective; (c) Control procedure

Task 8

(a) and (c)

Task 9

(a), (d) and (e) Investigate; (b) and (c) Accept

Task 10

(c) When the population is very small and all the items are material

Task 11

(a) Test of control; (b) Analytical procedure; (c) Test of detail

Task 12

(a) Cut-off; (b) Classification; (c) Accuracy

Task 13

Answer should include some or all of the following:

Attend Jellybean Ltd's inventory count and:

- observe the client's staff carrying out the count in accordance with their instructions

- note any deviation from inventory count instructions for later discussion with the client's management

- select a sample of items and count them independently for comparison with the client's count

- ensure that all items checked are detailed on audit working papers, together with any observed problems with the count

- if any tests prove unsatisfactory, request a recount be performed by the auditors and client staff

- where boxed goods are stored in stacks, ensure the stacks are complete and not hollow

- ask the client's staff to open a sample number of boxes to ensure the contents are as stated on the label

- note any damaged, obsolete or slow-moving inventory to ensure that these are separately identified and can be appropriately valued

- make a note of the count sheet numbers to ensure that all sheets are accounted for

- select a sample of the client's completed inventory count sheets and take a copy for comparison with the final versions used for inventory valuation

- note details of the last delivery of items into inventory and the last issue from inventory – details of the last delivery note or goods received note number should be recorded

Check valuation of inventory:

- check a sample of inventory values with original purchase documentation eg invoices

- review sales after year-end to ensure goods have not been sold at a value less than they cost

- carry out analytical review procedures to test the inventory valuation

Check cut off:

- review purchase invoices entered in to the client's accounting records shortly before and after the year-end and match them to the GRN to ensure that they have been recorded in the correct accounting period

- review GRNs issued after the year-end to ensure that none of these have been included in inventory or trade payables for the current financial period

- check records of goods returned to suppliers before the year end to ensure that any credit notes due have been received or accrued for

- check sales invoices before and after the year-end to ensure that goods despatched to customers have been invoiced in the correct accounting period

Task 14

(b)   95494, 94496 and 94497

Task 15

(a) and **(c)** Audit software; **(b)** Test data

Task 16

(a) Decrease risk; **(b)** and **(c)** Increase risk

Task 17

(a)   Inventory count

(b)   Purchase orders

Task 18

(a) and **(b)** are true; **(c)** is false

Task 19

(a) Does not require to be adjusted; **(b)** and **(c)** require to be adjusted

Task 20

This is a comprehensive list of the tests of payroll so the answer should include a good selection of these tests.

audit tests

* review a sample of joiners in the year to ensure that they have been correctly recorded in the appropriate month

* review staff files to check that changes in personnel details have been promptly updated on the payroll system

* for a sample of employees:

    - check individual wages or salaries figures from the payroll schedules against individual personnel records to verify rates of pay or salary figures

    - re-perform calculation of gross pay and deductions (eg PAYE, NI, pension) to ensure the calculations are correct

    - ensure voluntary deductions (eg pension contributions) have been authorised by the member of staff

    - confirm existence of staff members by arranging to meet them

    - check details of hours worked from payroll records to individual timesheets or clock cards

    - ensure clock cards and timesheets have been approved

    - ensure all overtime payments have been approved

- re-perform commission and bonus calculations to ensure they are consistent with supporting documentation (eg sales schedules or approved bonus schemes) and ensure that they have been approved for payment

- where staff have been paid piecework, check the production figures on which the payments are based to ensure that the payments have been correctly calculated

- check the calculation of benefits

- confirm payment of net pay to the BACS summary or the cash payments summary

• review the wages control account and ensure that it is regularly reconciled and all outstanding items are investigated

• check payroll software to ensure that up-to-date income tax and national insurance rates are being used to calculate payroll figures

• check figures from the payroll summary to the nominal ledger

• for a sample of payments to HM Revenue & Customs:

- ensure that the amount paid agrees to the liability shown on the payroll schedule

- ensure that the payment was made to HM Revenue & Customs within the permitted period to clear the income tax and NI liability account

• for payment of cash wages, observe distribution of pay packets to employees to ensure that:

- each employee receives a pay packet and no more than one pay packet

- procedures are in place to ensure that cash payments are secure

- all wage packets are signed for by members of staff

- a record is kept of unclaimed wages

- explanations are obtained for unclaimed wages

analytical procedures for payroll

As part of their testing, the auditors may carry out some analytical procedures as follows:
• comparing wages and salaries month-by-month with previous year figures
• comparing average salary per employee with previous year figures
• review increases in pay rates by comparison with previous year's payroll figures – eg if pay rises were generally 4% during the year, is the current wages and salaries figure approximately 4% greater than last year's figure?

Task 21

(a) and (c)

Task 22

Not significant

Task 23

Task 23	Consequences	Recommendations
The company does not have any procedures for approving suppliers	The suppliers used by Whoppa Ltd may not be the most competitive for quality and service These suppliers may no longer be financially secure Whoppa Ltd's dependence on a limited number of suppliers may put the continuity of supplies at risk if one or more of these suppliers has difficulties	The performance of all suppliers to the company should be reviewed regularly The company should invite a wide range of suppliers to tender for a supply contract All potential suppliers should be required to demonstrate their ability to continue to trade for the term of the contract
Purchase orders are always sent to the same few suppliers	The company may not be obtaining the best prices Suppliers may become complacent and the quality of products and services they supply may decline Relationships may develop between these suppliers and the staff who order goods. This may lead to staff being too friendly with suppliers and not challenging prices or quality. It could also lead to suppliers trying to bribe staff to maintain the flow of orders	Client staff should be rotated so they do not build up close relationships with individual suppliers Suppliers' performance should be monitored. Poor service should be challenged Suppliers' prices should be regularly compared with other suppliers' prices to ensure that Whoppa Ltd continues to buy goods at the best price

Task 24

(a) and (b) Substantive procedure; (c) Test of control

Task 25

Bing Ltd	(a)	Not modified
Bong Ltd	(e)	Adverse opinion – pervasive disagreement (Going concern)
Bang Ltd	(b)	'Except for' – limitation of scope (Unable to verify existence of assets)

Task 26

(a)   Do nothing, except continue to pursue the Sales Director. To go any further would breach your duty of confidentiality to your client

(You have no evidence that bribes are actually being paid. Until you can clarify the situation with the Sales Director you cannot breach client confidentiality.)

Task 27

    (b)   Makes the management accountable to the shareholders

Task 28

(a) False (Auditors can limit their liability under a claim for negligence **only by agreement with the shareholders**)

(b) True

Task 29

    (d)   Issuing International Accounting Standards (this is carried out by the IAASB)

Task 30

There is an **increase** in control risk in ALL cases.

Task 31

    (a)   The level of materiality is a matter for professional judgement

Task 32

(a) Open; **(b)** Closed; **(c)** Reflective

**Practice
assessment 2
answers**

Task 1

(a) Strong; (b) Weak

Task 2

(a) Risk; (b) Control procedure; (c) Control objective

Task 3

(a) and (c) No reliance; (b) Reliance

Task 4

(c)   Assignments to carry out the first audit of a new company on behalf of shareholders

Task 5

(a) Checklist; (b) Flowchart

Task 6

(a) Reduce; (b) and (c) Increase

Task 7

(a) Poor cash management; (b) Risk of failing to process customer orders; (c) Risk of non-payment for goods

Task 8

(a) Significant weakness; (b) and (c) Strength

Task 9

(a) and (b) Effect; (c) No effect

Task 10

(a)   Non-current asset register

(b)   Goods received records

Task 11

(a) and (c) Substantive procedure; (b) Test of control

Task 12

(b) and (c)

Task 13

(1) **Risks**

- Inappropriate split between current and non-current liabilities

- Incomplete disclosure in the notes to the financial statements

- Going concern risk if company fails to comply with the terms of the loan

- Inflation of profits to ensure compliance with the interest cover requirement

(2) **Procedures**

- Inspect loan agreement for terms and conditions

- Direct confirmation with lender of balance outstanding at the year end

- Vouch loan repayments and interest to bank statements and cash book

- Re-perform the calculation of the split between current and non-current liabilities

- Inspect notes to the financial statements to ensure disclosures in respect of the terms are complete

- Examine cash flow forecasts to ensure loan obligations can be met in the future

- Examine profit forecasts to ensure interest cover can be maintained in the foreseeable future

Task 14

(a) Cut-off; **(b)** Classification; **(c)** Accuracy

Task 15

(a) and **(c)** Audit software; **(b)** Test data

Task 16

(a) and **(c)** Increase risk of misstatement; **(b)** Reduces risk of misstatement

Task 17

(a) Weakness; **(b)** Strength

Task 18

(a) False; **(b)** and **(c)** True

Task 19

(b)   The adjustment is not material so the value of finished goods inventory does not need to be adjusted

Task 20

- Vouch a sample of entries for materials to invoices
- Vouch a sample of entries for wages/salaries to payroll records
- Trace a sample of invoices to costing records
- Trace a sample of timesheet/payroll details to the costing records
- Re-perform the overhead percentage calculation
- For a sample of contracts in progress at the year end compare actual costs:
    - To contract price to identify losses
    - To budget to identify cost overruns and potential losses

Task 21

No further action

Task 22

Refer to supervisor

Task 23

(1) **Consequences**

- Equipment recorded in the register may not exist or may have been stolen
- Equipment in existence, acquisitions or disposals may not be recorded
- Equipment may be fully written down but still in use
- Equipment may be impaired and consequently overvalued
- Depreciation charges on the equipment may be inappropriate

(2) **Recommendations**

- Periodic reconciliation of:
    - Physical equipment to register to ensure completeness of recording
    - Entries in the register to physical equipment to ensure existence and in good condition
- Reconciliation to be performed independent of custodian
- Differences to be reported and investigated
- Monitoring of procedures to ensure checks undertaken

Task 24

(b) Include in report to management only

Task 25

Requires to be adjusted

Task 26

(c)   Report the fraud to the directors of Puffers plc and await their response

Task 27

'The objectives of the auditor are:

(a)   To identify and **assess** the risks of **material** misstatement of the financial statements due to fraud;

(b)   To obtain sufficient **appropriate** audit evidence regarding the assessed risks of material misstatement due to fraud, through designing and implementing appropriate responses

Task 28

(a) is False; **(b)** is True

Task 29

The IAASB is responsible for: **(d)** Setting auditing standards which facilitate the convergence of national and international auditing standards

Task 30

(a) and **(b)** Decrease; **(c)** Increase

Task 31

(a) is True; **(b)** is False

Task 32

(a) Closed; **(b)** Open; **(c)** Reflective

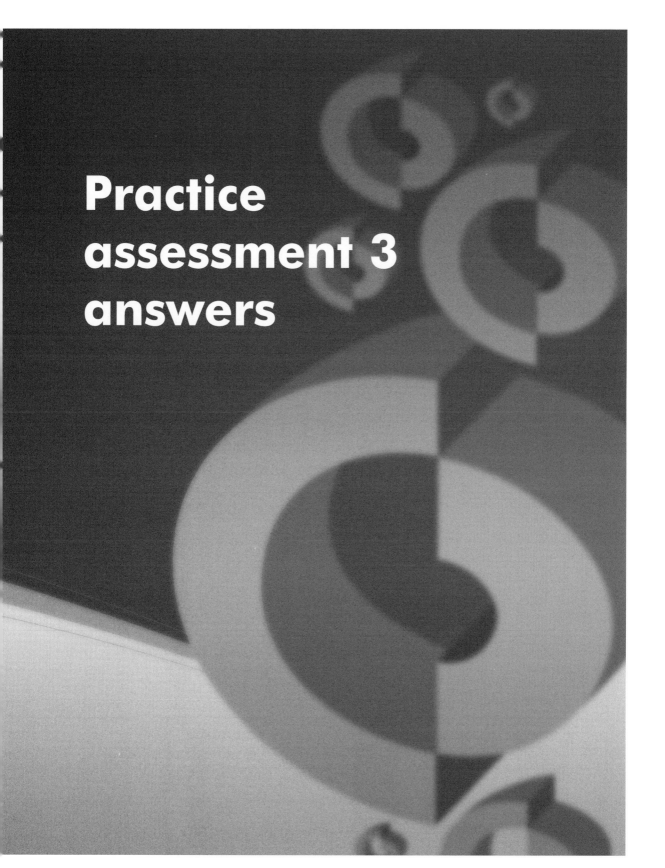

Practice assessment 3 answers

Task 1

> **(a)** and **(c)** are False; **(b)** is True.

Task 2

> **(a)** Risk of paying for goods not ordered
>
> **(b)** Risk of ordering excessive amounts of goods

Task 3

> **(a)** and **(c)** Decrease; **(b)** Increase

Task 4

> (d)   None of the above

Task 5

> **(a)** and **(c)** are Lack of control; **(b)** is Control

Task 6

> **(a)** and **(b)** Increase; **(c)** Decrease

Task 7

> **(a)** (1); **(b)** (2); **(c)** (5)

Task 8

> **(a)** Weakness; **(b)** Strength

Task 9

> (a) and (d)

Task 10

> **(a)** Increase; **(b)** and **(c)** Decrease

Task 11

> BOTH statements are True.

Task 12

> (c)   Ask the Company Accountant to confirm the existence of all employees on the payroll

Task 13

Audit risks

- Price of materials – include delivery charges and costs where not otherwise recovered (e.g. VAT)
- Labour costs should be included at actual cost to the business not charge-out rate, this may require adjustment
- Costs based on hours worked at actual pay rate plus NI etc
- Only direct labour should be included – there should be no inclusion of costs relating to other staff not working on the project
- Only direct overheads relating to the project should be included – no proportion of administrative or selling and delivery overheads to be included
- The new building should be independently valued to ensure value is not lower than the costs incurred and included in the non-current asset figure

Task 14

(d)   Performing a walk through test of the revenue system

Task 15

(a) is True; (b) is False

Task 16

(a) and (b) Increase risk of misstatement; (c) Reduce risk of misstatement

Task 17

(a) Provides assurance; (b) Does not provide assurance

Task 18

(a) and (c) True; (b) False

Task 19

(a) and (d) take no further action; (b), (c) and (e) refer to supervisor

Task 20

Existence and ownership

- Verify documentation relating to origin of asset
- Confirm the asset is not time limited and with an end date
- Request third party confirmation of existence and ownership from lawyers
- Inspect any certificates and third party documentation
- For purchased goodwill inspect contracts etc relating to creation of asset
- Ascertain details of royalty payments etc and match to underlying documentation

Completeness

- Review legal documentation

Value

- Ensure the asset, for example, patent, trademark, is still current and write off over useful life
- Goodwill – ensure underlying value amortised correctly
- Consider estimated useful life of purchased goodwill and any permanent diminution in value
- Value of brands – these cannot be capitalised if they were created internally. Only those purchased can be capitalised so review current viability of brand identity
- If necessary use external valuers and consultants to value intangible assets
- Ensure the client has tested its intangible assets for impairment

Task 21

(b) An invoice for 'Consultancy Advice' addressed to a company based in Panama

(d) An invoice for the sale of goods addressed to the Finance Director showing a 50% discount on normal prices

Task 22

Significant

Task 23

Issues

- Segregation of duties – two members of staff do everything and consequently the whole process
- Lack of management supervision
- Direct links with warehouse could lead to possible collusion
- Possible exposure of the business to theft and fraud
- Possible collusion with suppliers

Recommendations

- Allocate specific tasks to individuals
- Increased management involvement – for example prices and discounts should be negotiated by management
- Remove certain tasks from the members of staff, for example entry into financial records could be transferred to accounts
- Ensure orders that have been placed are confirmed in writing and matched with goods received records and invoices
- Use suppliers statements to reconcile balances monthly and return documentation
- Faulty goods should be returned by managers and not warehouse staff to ensure bona fide claims against suppliers

Task 24

Significant

Task 25

Modified opinion

Task 26

Not appropriate

Task 27

(a) and (c) Management objective; (b) External audit objective

Task 28

(c)   Including the Bannerman wording in the audit report

Task 29

(b)   Auditors are permitted to deviate from the requirements of ISAs in exceptional circumstances provided they can justify their actions

Task 30

(a) increases audit risk; **(b)** reduces audit risk

Task 31

(b) and **(d)** are material; **(a)** and **(c)** are not material

Task 32

(a) Open; **(b)** and **(c)** Closed; **(d)** Reflective

for your notes

for your notes

for your notes

for your notes

for your notes

for your notes